RUBE REMEMBERS:

Tales of a Yell County Country Boy

❖

Rubin Reed &
Bunny Reed Woods

Illustrated by: Melody M. Henry

THE
Write
CONNECTION
Jackson, Tennessee

Produced by The Write Connection, 67 Channing
Way, Jackson, Tennessee 38305.

Pre-assigned LCCN: 98-61632
ISBN: 0-7392-0052-6

Printed in the United States of America by:
Morris Publishing ❖ 3212 East Highway 30 ❖ Kearney, NE 68847

DEDICATION

To Bunny, without whom there
would be no book,
and to Lillian, without whom there
would be no story.
—Rubin Reed

To my dad, Rube Reed,
the most fascinating storyteller I have
ever known. You are among the finest
of fathers. It is my desire that
families will enjoy *reading* this book
together as much as you and I have
enjoyed *writing* it together.
Thank you, Dad, for the privilege of
working on this project with you.
—Bunny Reed Woods

ACKNOWLEDGMENT

We'd like to acknowledge thanks to the following people for their friendship and support in the compilation of this book:

Herman Aikman, Inez Aikman, Mr. Baker, Chester Blocker, Joe Brown, Charles Dickson, Hoyt Dixon, Rev. Peter Emery, Roy Forest, Knox Jones, Clinton Hayston, Ivory Hayston, Melody M. Henry, Marie Kenner, Charlie Kitchen, Jimmy Ladd, Amanda Mathis, Tom Mathis, Ervin Millwood, Joe Mitchell, Cecil McCormick, Ben Montgomery, Ida Montgomery, Butch Patton, Berline Patton, George Patton, Lorene Pelt, Nina Jean Parshley, Robert Parshley, Rev. Dennis Phillips, Odessa Quails, Afton Ratliff, Albert Reed, Billy Reed, Carl Reed, Cinda Reed, Darrell Reed, Hattie Pearl Reed, Herb Reed, Idell Reed, James Mitchell (Jim) Reed, Jim Reed, Rev. Jesse Reed, Johnny Reed, Lee Harriett Samantha (Hattie) Reed, Lena Reed, Lillian Reed, Lorene Reed, Mike Reed, Norma Reed, Ola Reed, Odell Reed, Roy Reed, Roy E. Reed, Ship Reed, Jimmy Reeve, LeAndra Smith, Reneé Smith, Smitty Smith, Rev. Will Smith, Genevia Swain, Gilbert Swain, Gilmer Swain, Girty Swain, Girthy Swain, Glidy Swain, Grover Swain, Gurn Swain, Guss Swain, Jody Swain, Ottis Swain, Rev. Homer Wehunt, Rev. R. L. Whitten, Clebert Wood, Gary Woods, and Rev. George Young.

FOREWORD

I used to think I would like to be a writer. I still think if I'd had a better education and the proper training, I could have been one.

In 1991 my daughter, Bunny, gave me a journal. She told me that if I decided to write anything in it, she would be glad to have it. So I did. I told her my spelling was rough, though, and I trusted she wouldn't laugh at it any. (Wouldn't you know it'd be just my luck that Bunny made a school teacher?)

ILLUSTRATIONS

❖ All illustrations in this book were drawn by
   Melody M. Henry of Jackson, Tennessee.

CONTENTS

❖ **1** ❖

***Figure 1.1 "The Swimming Hole
at Reed Creek"***

❖ 1 ❖

GROWING UP

I was born in Aly, Arkansas (located in Yell County) on July 2, 1918 to James Mitchell & Lee Harriet Samantha (Hattie) Reed. I have heard my mother say I ruined her 4th of July picnic by coming on July 2nd. They always had a community picnic on July 4th. Uncle Jackson made two big tubs of lemonade for the picnic. Everyone had fun.

I was named Rubin Vessie Reed. I never liked the name Vessie. All of my life I have been called "Rube," except when my parents or teachers wanted to scold me. Then it was "RU-BIN!" (stressed).

I had ten brothers and sisters: Ola, Roy, Herb, Odell, Idell, Jesse, Carl, Lorene, Billy, and Lena. Being in the middle of eleven children (seven boys and four girls), I was spoiled by my older brothers and sisters.

I remember complaining about having to help raise the younger ones. My older brother, Jesse, would do something and tell Mom and Dad that my sister, Idell, or I did it. Mom and Dad would spank me and Idell, then Jesse would laugh at us. We never could spank Jesse.

Dad was a deacon long, long before I was born, and he and Mother saw to it we were in Sunday school and church every Sunday. I'm glad they did, because all the children turned out to be Christians. My mom and dad taught all of us children to work and to respect everyone. Mother always taught the Golden Rule: Treat others as you would have them treat you. Dad always taught truth and honesty. He said, "If you tell the truth, then when you tell it again later, it's *so* much easier to remember."

My thirteen years at Aly were full of excitement. There was never a dull moment at our house.

Learning to Swim

Dad taught all seven boys to swim at a very early age—usually around six years. We lived between two creeks, and Dad said he knew if he didn't teach us to swim, some of us would drown. Mother wouldn't let the girls go. Dad had a pine pole about six feet long with the bark peeled off of it. He would put his chin and the boy's chin over it and paddle around. The pole would float and keep the child from sinking. When Dad saw the boy could swim, he would go in water over the boy's head, push the pole out from underneath their chins, and say, "Now let's swim to the banks together." It worked.

The Swain family were our closest neighbors. You could almost throw a rock from our house to theirs. Our farms had a narrow lane between them. Jody and Ottis Swain had nine children (five boys and four girls). All nine of their names started with "g": Grover, Girty, Guss, Gurn, Girthy, Glidy, Gilbert, Gilmer, and Genevia. I never knew if they planned it that way or not. We Reed and Swain children grew up like brothers and sisters. The Reed children would mind Jody and Ottis and the Swain children would mind Jim and Hattie.

Reed Creek ran through our farm and we had a big swimming hole that got a lot of activity. We both had cows and calves, and we both had a calf pasture with a water pond. In the summer time the ponds would dry up and we children would drive the calves down this lane to water. We Reed boys would get there first, pull our clothes off, and go swimming naked. The Swain girls would drive their calves down and watch the Reed boys swim. My big brother, Herb, would swim like a dolphin, duck his head under, and make his butt come out of the water. One day he did that and Girty giggled and said, "Herbie, let's see you do that again."

Mama stepped out from behind a big tree and said, "Yes, Herb. Let's see you do *that* again!" Needless to say, that broke up the party.

Surviving Close Calls

We lived a mile and a half from school. When the weather was bad, we children would ride horses to school. One day a big snow was on the ground. My sister, Idell, was riding a little black stallion and a neighbor boy threw his coat over the horse's head. The stallion threw Idell and her foot hung in a stirrup. The horse ran away, dragging her in the snow. Cecil McCormick (a grown man) got on his chestnut horse, out-ran the little black stallion, and saved Idell's life.

When I was nine years old, my dad and older brothers would go logging. When Jesse and I would hear them coming down the muddy road, we would run down and meet them. Then we would ride the cupling pole. One day I fell off the cupling pole and my head went down into a deep, muddy rut. The back wheel of the wagon ran over my head and almost killed me. It dislocated bone structure in my nose and I never could breathe correctly through my right nostril again. (At the age of thirty-eight I had surgery and corrected it.)

My grandpa and grandma lived half a mile from us. I used to spend the night with them. He would fix himself a little whisky and water with sugar before breakfast. My grandpa was ninety-six when he died. He might have made it to one hundred if he had left an old mule alone. The mule pawed my grandpa while he was feeding it. As a result, he spent the last four years in a wheelchair.

Telling Animal Stories

We boys hunted and fished a lot. We had a big red dog named Taft. He would tree about anything that left a scent. A preacher named Wehunt had a big family and preached for us at Aly. He always brought his family to our house. He liked to eat fried squirrel.

One day we Reed boys killed fourteen red squirrels and four young coons. Mom fried the four young coons and set them in front of the preacher. (Brother Wehunt had told Mom he couldn't eat coon, on account of the taste.) He had eaten half of his plateful when Mom told him it was coon. He replied, "Sister Reed, I don't believe you, because that was the biggest and best fox squirrel I ever ate." Finally, we showed him the four coon hides and he had to believe Mom.

❖ ❖ ❖

At another time a distant relative, Ship Reed, brought his wife and children by. The boy named Darrell came up in the woods where old Taft had a squirrel treed. We were shooting at the squirrel with our bean shooters. One of us hit the squirrel and it sailed out of the tree. Darrell caught the squirrel as if he were catching a ball. The squirrel bit Darrell through his hand, and he had to choke it to death before he could get the squirrel's teeth out.

The squirrel had a decent burial, though. Since I wanted to be a preacher when I grew up, I performed funeral services for pets and special animals in the community. I would stand on a stump and preach my heart out, while my brothers, sisters, and neighboring children would sing the special music. (I had learned to imitate four different preachers from our community: Peter Emery, Will Smith, Homer Wehunt, and Dennis Philips.)

❖   ❖   ❖

Gurn's brother, Gib, used to take me squirrel hunting. When his dog treed a squirrel, I would shake a bush on the other side of the tree to turn the squirrel so Gib could shoot it. One day the dog treed a small animal in a hollow log. Gib looked into the hollow log, grinned, and said, "Oh, it's an old 'possum."

Someone had chopped a hole about eight feet from the end of the log. A big stick was lying near it. Gib said, "I'll hold old Red at the hole, and you punch the stick and push the 'possum out. Then I'll let old Red catch her."

I put the stick in and punched about three times, and a skunk filled my face full of it. The skunk ran out of the hole. The dog jerked loose from Gib, caught the skunk, and slung it all over Gib. The trick back-fired on him. All of us were sick.

❖ **2** ❖

**Figure 2.1 "The One-room Schoolhouse
in Aly, Arkansas"**

❖2❖

SCHOOL DAYS

School Days in Aly

My first years of school were in Aly, Arkansas. We didn't have a toilet at the one-room schoolhouse, so all of us boys went behind a big tree to go to the restroom. After about four years an overdose of acid killed the tree.

My First School Teacher

My first school teacher was a neighbor boy named Gurn Swain. He told me the day before school started that if I didn't behave in school, he was going to beat the s--- out of me. Well, I pulled Marie Kenner's hair and she cried. Gurn hollered at me, "What did I tell you?" I grinned and loudly repeated what Gurn had said to me earlier—word for word. A rather embarrassed Gurn spanked me, then turned his head to keep me from seeing him laugh.

If I did something the teacher needed to spank me for, Gurn would say, "Now Rube, remind me to spank you when school is out." As soon as school was dismissed I would grab my coat, start running, and throw small rocks at Gurn. He always caught up with me and then I got it. He never did spank me hard enough to hurt, and he always had to turn his head to keep me from seeing him laugh.

One day I got into trouble, and when school was out Gurn walked home with me. When I got a spanking at school, it always meant I got another one at home. Some of the other children had beaten us home and told Mama, so Mama was standing on the front porch waiting for me. Gurn looked up at her, then shook his head and grinned and said, "Aunt Hat, please don't spank him—he's had three today already."

Chester Blocker and I got more spankings than all the other children put together. One time Chester Blocker did something on a Friday and Gurn said, "Chester, remind me to spank you when school is out." When school was out,

Chester grabbed his coat and started running as fast as he could. Gurn yelled after him, "Chester, come back here and take your spanking!"

Chester replied over his quickly disappearing shoulder, "I'll just wait 'til Monday and take both of them!"

❖　　❖　　❖

We had a drinking well at school which had a big curbing around the top of it. One day I was playing on the well curbing and caught a blue-bellied lizard. A big girl named Odessa Quails walked by and I put the lizard down her dress. She chased me down and tied me up with a piece of barbed wire. It scratched me up pretty badly. Gurn didn't spank me for that. I guess he thought being tied up with barbed wire was punishment enough.

My Second School Teacher

My second teacher was a lady named Lorene Pelt. She was a good teacher. One day when Ervin Millwood (a big boy) was on the stage reciting his lesson, I got his bottle of blue ink and painted some blue shoes on my bare feet. The teacher made me sit on the table up front and show everyone my pretty shoes. When I got home, my mother couldn't spank me. She had to turn her head to laugh.

**Figure 2.2 "The Blue-bellied Lizard
on the Well Curbing"**

School Days

My Third School Teacher

My third teacher was Dwayne Gloster. He entered me in a track meet and I outran everyone. He grabbed me up in his arms and called me his boy. I really liked Dwayne until one day when his horse threw him. I saw a bottle of whiskey he had and found out he was drunk.

My Fourth School Teacher

My fourth teacher was Tom Mathis. Tom was one of the finest men I have ever known. He should have spanked me one time, but didn't. One Sunday afternoon when Hoyt Dixon and I were playing in the schoolhouse, I wrote on the blackboard and forgot to erase it. It said, "Monkey and baboon sitting in the grass. Baboon said, 'I see your a--.' " Monday morning it was still up there. Everyone saw it before the teacher did. Tom knew it was my writing. He just grinned and made me erase it. It was embarrassing, but I got over it.

Tom and Amanda lived at Whittley, which is now Briggsville. One weekend Tom took me home with him and I had a good time. Amanda used to come and pick peas, and I always filled her up on watermelons afterwards. Tom and Amanda didn't have any children. I asked Amanda if the weekend she took care of me caused her to not want children. She made me feel good when she answered, "Rube, I would've liked to have had a little tyke like you."

My Fifth School Teacher

My fifth teacher was Charles Dickson. He had lost a leg just below his knee and had made himself a wooden leg. He put his knee in on some padding and strapped the wooden piece to his upper leg. One stick came up to his waist and then strapped around his waist. He was like family, because he married a neighbor girl, Girthy Swain. He could outrun all of us children, even with his wooden leg.

School Days in Tippey Town

We moved away from Aly and our old log house where Mother had us eleven children. My next years of school were in a place between Rover and Plainview called Tippey Town, Arkansas. They were all farmers and all good people.

My time at Tippey Town and Plainview school was very rewarding. The houseful of Reed children went to our new consolidated school the very first day. It was exciting not having to look at one teacher all day. Instead, we had one for each class period and one for study hall.

School Days

First Day at the New School

The boys at the new school wanted to see if the Reed boys were sissies, so they paired us up with boys our own size and made us fight. We all won and became rather well-accepted. They paired me with a guy named Jimmy Ladd. Jimmy had had polio and had a lame leg. I had broken my right wrist, so they paired two cripples. Well, I first happened to get a good left hook to Jimmy's nose. When it was all over, we became best of buddies and are still good friends in our old days.

Jimmy and I often spent the night with each other. He had never shot a shotgun. I had been shooting one since I was nine years old. Jimmy kept wanting to fire my shotgun. Even though Jimmy was bigger than I was, I told him it took a big boy to shoot it. Finally, I let him shoot it. My shotgun kicked a tooth through Jimmy's lip, bloodied his nose, and hurt his shoulder.

Home Cooking and Home Brew

We got a baseball team started in Tippey Town. My brothers, Jesse and Odell, and I were on the team. I believe we could have had a career in baseball, but Dad said baseball was a waste of time. Dad said we had to stay at home and cut the winter's wood, put up hay and fodder, and pick peas. This was in the middle of the big Depression, and times were hard. We had plenty to eat, but not much money. We grew about all our food. We always had plenty of pork, beef, chickens, rabbits, and vegetables.

We had some good rabbit dogs, so we killed and ate a lot of swamp rabbits. One day we were rabbit hunting and the dogs were running. Ivory and Clinton Hayston were with me. I had to go to the bathroom and crawled up on a stump. About the time I got through, the dogs ran the rabbit by me. I was using the old shotgun that Jimmy Ladd shot. I shot the rabbit and the shotgun kicked me backward off the stump. (It was messy.) Ivory and Clinton never let me live that one down.

Mom had two ten-gallon stone jars she made sour-kraut in. When she was finished with them, we boys would take them to a spring under the hill and make home brew. Our little brother, Billy, caused us to get caught. Billy caught us bottling the home brew and told us that if we didn't give him some of it, he was going to tell Mom and Dad. We gave him two tin cups of it, and thought we had all our bases covered.

What we didn't count on was that in a round-about way, Billy's little body wound up telling on us anyway. While eating his supper that night, Billy fell out of his chair twice. When our large family went to the big room after supper, Billy climbed up on our organ stool that went round and round, became dizzy, and slid off of it. Even that wouldn't have been so bad, except that he slid right smack between Mom's feet. When Mom picked him up, Billy burped in her face. That's when it hit the fan. Dad found the home brew and poured all of it out. Then Dad told us if we ever made home brew again, he would turn us over to the sheriff.

We moved the home brew to Uncle Jimmy Reeve's sorghum mill. Then we dug a big hole in the plummy pile (stalks of sorghum cane with juice squeezed out of it, which kept it from rotting for a long time). We made another batch of home brew out of sorghum juice and it almost killed us. Our mother found out about the still. She and Mrs. Swain took their axes and chopped our still to pieces. That completely ended our making home brew.

Good Friends and Onery Neighbors

Good Friends: R.L. Whitten

I had a good buddy named R. L. Whitten. We rode horses all the time. One day I found a yellow jacket nest in our pasture. When R. L.

and I went riding the next time, I took him to the spot and moved my horse around until his pony stood over the yellow jacket nest. Pretty soon, his pony started kicking and stomping and switching her tail. When old Daisy started backing and ran away with R. L., she got tangled up in a bunch of buck vines. R. L. could have gotten hurt. I have always been sorry I did that. R. L. made a preacher and a school teacher.

Good Friends: Nina Jean Parshley

I thought I was old enough to join the big boys when I saved Nina Jean Parshley from drowning in the river in 1931. Several families of children had a favorite swimming hole on the river. A big flat rock served as a ledge. On one side the rock dropped off into only four feet of water, but on the opposite side it dropped off into eight feet of water.

One summer day we children were playing at this swimming hole when Nina Jean fell off the rock ledge into the deep part of the water. Nina Jean couldn't swim. I quickly jumped in and dove straight down, getting her by the ankles. I planted my feet on the muddy bottom and pushed Nina Jean up to the surface. Her brother, Robert, was able to pull her to safety from there.

School Days

Good Friends: My Brother, Carl

While living at Tippey Town my brother, Carl, broke an ankle. Mom didn't want Carl to miss school, but it was a small distance from our house to the school bus stop. Mom made Jesse and me pull Carl in a little red wagon three-fourths of a mile to catch the bus in the morning, and then three-fourths of a mile back home in the afternoon. This went on for *months*. Jesse and I knew good and well that Carl could walk by then.

We had a neighbor who had a bunch of old hound dogs. The dogs were always having fits. One day Jesse and I were pulling Carl in the little wagon. Just before we got to Parsley's house, one of those dogs took a fit and someone hollered, "A mad dog!" Jesse and I dropped the wagon tongue and ran to the nearest house. Guess what? Old Carl passed us before we got there. We made Carl pull the little red wagon home and never transported him to and from the school bus stop again.

Onery Neighbors

Onery Neighbors: Rex Milfin

We children would hire out for other farmers when we got caught up on our cotton picking. One day four families of children were picking cotton for Mr. Clifford Milfin. Rex Milfin, a nephew of Clifford's, was a big, fat, lazy boy. If he sat still for a few minutes, he would go to sleep.

We used to carry our lunch in half-gallon sorghum buckets. One day after lunch the chickens were eating our leftovers. Rex fell asleep and started snoring, and we all laughed at him. I got a stick and put some fresh chicken crap on his right hand and tickled his upper lip with a straw. At first he tried to blow what he thought was a fly off of his lip. After that didn't work, Rex raked his right hand across his lip and filled both nostrils with the chicken crap.

Needless to say, Rex woke up in a hurry and started chasing me. I was small and could run fast, but he could run too. He chased me through three barbed wire fences. He would get close and I would slide under the fence. It took Rex a while to get through, so I would gain on him. He never caught me. Four years later I stayed with him and Froggie Johnson and picked cotton at Lepanto, Arkansas. He would look at me and grin and say, "You little whitehead, I still ought to wring your neck for that." It was a dirty trick, but everyone—well, everyone except Rex—had a good laugh.

School Days

Onery Neighbors: Harry Trell

There was a big, mean man named Harry Trell who lived across the field from us. He plowed up our road every time he plowed his cotton, and our old Model-T Ford would almost shake our liver out when we went over it. Dad asked Harry to quit it, but he kept on.

One day I brought a brand-new baseball bat to a game. (I had chopped cotton for fifty cents a day to purchase it.) Harry Trell picked up my new bat and deliberately broke it. When I called Harry a hog-jawed so-and-so, he slapped me about ten feet. I sat there thinking Harry was going to kick me all the way to the Arkansas/Tennessee state line. My brother, Jesse, came running with his fists up and instructed, "Sit still, Rube. I'll take care of him!"

As I said, Harry was a big, big, man— about 275 or 300 pounds. He smirked and told Jesse, "You little whippersnapper, I'll knock your head off."

Well, the fight began. Harry swung at Jesse and Jesse ducked. When Harry swung around Jesse, Jesse hit the big man in the face about four times. We bystanders called out to Harry, "So when are you going to start 'knocking his head off,' huh?" This whole process was repeated over and over.

Rube Remembers

Big Harry's nose was bleeding, a tooth was almost cut through his lip, and one of his eyes was black. (The rest of his body didn't look too good, either.) When Harry kicked at Jesse, Jesse grabbed his foot, twisted it, and threw him to the ground. Big Harry was whipped and started crawling off on his hands and knees. Jesse ran up and kicked him in the butt and said, "That's what you get for plowing up our road!" It was a case of a big, fat bully who was too slow to hit a guy one-third his weight. (Jesse, who never grew taller than 5' 7", went on to become a well-known preacher who also served as Director of Missions and Evangelism in Arkansas for over thirty years.) Harry Trell didn't buy me a new bat, but he soon moved away and we got a better neighbor.

Onery Neighbors: Roy Libbord

We had a good milk cow named Lady, and our big family depended on her for milk. Our milk cow started coming home with no milk. Dad thought some big calves in the pasture were drinking all Lady's milk, so he followed her. Roy Libbord, a guy who didn't like to work much, lived down the hill from us. Dad found Roy sitting on a stool, milking Lady. Dad walked up behind him and said, "Milk enough for me too, Roy. She hasn't been bringing me any." Well, old Roy moved that night.

Onery Neighbors: Gifford Wifcott

The next neighbor made a path through our corn patch to keep from walking a quarter of a mile around the road. As the man went across our corn patch, he would fill his pockets with corn. Dad didn't say anything to him, because the man had a bunch of hungry children.

However, Dad did set a trap for another neighbor, Gifford Wifcott. Gifford wouldn't work much. It was told on him that once when a neighbor offered Gifford a bushel of corn so his children could have some food, Gifford asked, "Are the ears of corn shucked?" and Phil replied, "No," so Gifford turned down the food and said, "Well, just drive on." Boy, was he lazy!

Gifford was swiping Dad's corn to feed his hogs. Dad had had about enough, so he marked several ears of corn by pushing pine splinters into the cobs. Then Dad left the marked ears where Gifford had been helping himself to Dad's corn. One day when Dad and Mr. Swain were looking at Gifford's hogs, Dad broke a few corncobs and found some with the pine splinters in them. Dad didn't say anything to Mr. Swain, but later he showed these marked corncobs to Gifford and said, "All I ask is that you plant some corn next year and bring back what you took." Well, Gifford planted some corn, but I don't know if he brought any back.

Onery Neighbors: Alias, "Dad Wurner"

Most of the folks in Tippey Town had lived in the community since before they could remember. However, Tippey Town did have one newcomer in the early 1930's. There was an old man with a long, dark beard who called himself "Dad Wurner." Dad Wurner lived in the area for several years. When he became ill, his neighbors, Mr. and Mrs. Jones, took care of him. On his deathbed, Dad Wurner told the Jones family that his real name was Cole Younger. These words caused quite a bit of excitement in the community. Cole Younger had been a member of the Jesse James Gang!

School Days in Briggsville

Meeting Lillian

In 1934 we moved to Briggsville, formerly Whittley. The first day we Reed children went to the Fourche Valley School, a big snow was on the ground. A bunch of boys put us Reed boys to the test to see if we were sissies. They ganged up on us and snowballed us. I got behind the agricultural building and rolled a bunch of snowballs with rocks about the size of eggs inside of them. I threw one at a tall red-headed boy named Knox Jones. He saw it coming and ducked. It hit a pretty little dark-haired, round-faced girl right between the eyes and knocked her down. I ran over to her and blood was running down the front of her pretty blue coat. I thought I had knocked her eye out. She had seen me throw the snowball, so when I tried to help her up, she pushed me away and said, "Get away from me. I don't like you."

I got scolded by the superintendent, but he didn't spank me. My little sister, Lorene, was in the pretty girl's room at school. Lorene told Mom and Dad about the snowball episode. The pretty girl turned out to be Lillian Wood. Her parents and my parents grew up together and went to school together. Lillian finally accepted my apology after three weeks, and we started sitting together at school programs. We started dating a little and I knew I could really love her.

Driving a Model-T

At this time I drove a 1927 Model-T Roadster that was old and very slow. One day I was driving some friends to play in a baseball game. We came to a speed limit sign marked

"25 miles per hour." I floored the accelerator and exclaimed, "Hang on, gang—I think we can make it!"

Becoming a Christian

In 1932 twenty-seven young people in the Plainview community became Christians while attending a revival led by Charlie Kitchen. Jesse and I were part of that group. Jesse and I were baptized in Peavine Branch (near New Bible Bethel Missionary Baptist Church) by Rev. George Young. The water was only 1½ feet deep, so the preacher had to stand on his knees to baptize us. (That took some *real* dedication.)

Later, in 1953, I was ordained as a deacon. From that point on, I served as an active deacon in every church I attended until my health failed me.

Leaving Briggsville

We lived at Briggsville until January of 1936, then moved to Dumas. We lived on sixty acres at the end of Walnut Lake where it ran to 19 Canal. Dad and I farmed and made a good cotton crop. Dad made enough money to pay off two mortgages. Two years later he bought a little farm three miles west at Dumas. Mom lived to be seventy-two and Dad lived to be eighty-four.

Barber College Days in Denver

When the crop was harvested, I went to Byers, Colorado to visit my brother, who had a barber shop. I liked his set-up and enrolled in the State Barber College in Denver. When I finished my schooling, I worked for my brother, Herb. Well, old Rube made a barber and cut hair for fifty years. I cut my first head of hair October 4, 1936 and cut my last head of hair October 4, 1986.

I was eighteen years old and fit in with the high-schoolers, so I had a lot of fun and made many friends. I knew I liked Lillian a lot, but I couldn't be with her.

I fell in love with a cute little girl about Lillian's caliber named Lori Rockweller. Her mother was a nurse and her dad was a mail carrier. I could visualize Lori and I getting married and making our home in Colorado. One day Lori just doubled up and died. They never knew what was wrong with her. It knocked me for a loop. I was not happy at Byers anymore, so I moved back to Arkansas.

❖ **3** ❖

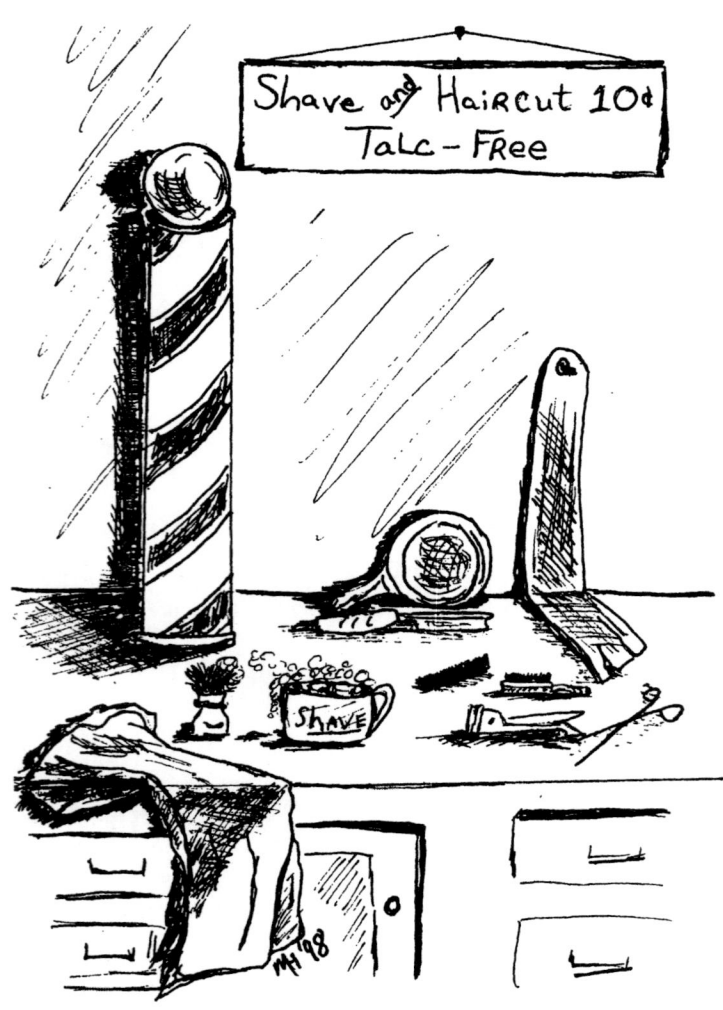

Figure 3.1 "Rube's Barber Shop"

❖ 3 ❖

STARTING A FAMILY

Marrying Lillian

When I returned to Arkansas, I began working in a barber shop in Ola. Lillian and I hadn't seen each other in over a year. One Friday afternoon a very quiet Lillian and her talkative mother came into the shop to visit for a while. I carried their luggage to the depot and they caught a train to Dumas. Sunday afternoon I met the train and carried Lillian's and her mom's luggage to the bus station. I asked Lillian if I could ride up to spend some time with her. Lillian said she would like that.

We started dating again, and I realized I really loved Lillian and wanted to spend the rest of my life with her. We were engaged in January of 1940 and married June 9, 1940. We didn't have a lot of extra money, so we were married in front of the headlights of a car. It doesn't take a fancy wedding to make a *real* marriage.

Having Our First Child

When we first married, we lived at Perryville, Arkansas. I ran a barber shop and pool hall. Later we moved to Hot Springs, where our first child, Bunny, was born. The doctor couldn't figure out why Lillian had a high fever trying to give birth. He finally put my wife to sleep. When the doctor came to the hospital the next morning, Lillian's jaws were swollen halfway over the pillow. She had the mumps. She was having so much trouble giving birth that the doctor thought the baby was dead. Although it was a forced delivery, Bunny was alive.

I had to sell my cow to pay the doctor bills for Bunny's birth. Horse racing was going on at Hot Springs and I had leased a barber shop about four blocks from the track. I thought I could make some money betting on the horses. I would close the barber shop and go to the track, then return and work half of the night. (Years later I moved back to Hot Springs, but I only went to the race track two times, and that was to get two loads of horse manure for my garden. I *still* say that if you could beat the races, they wouldn't be able to operate.)

Moving Our Family

We moved to Dumas and I worked in a barber shop there until the draft board guys told me that if I didn't get in essential work, I would be drafted. I left Dumas and worked in the shipyards in Wilmington, California. Next I worked on a ranch at Somis, California.

One day when I came home from working on the ranch in Somis, I saw a stray dog in our yard. I didn't want the dog around Bunny while she was playing outside, so I threw some rocks at the stray and let out a blue streak of bad words. The dog left, and I went inside for a few minutes.

When I went back outside, the dog was returning. To my surprise, three-year old Bunny was throwing rocks and yelling the *exact* same bad words I had yelled. That taught me a major lesson about my responsibility as a father. I cleaned up my speech after that!

I worked at the ranch in Somis for a short time. Before long, I was drafted into the Army.

❖ **4** ❖

Figure 4.1 "Target Practice in the Army"

❖ 4 ❖

ARMY DAYS

Army Days in Fort Chaffey

Receiving A True Army Welcome

I was inducted at Fort Chaffey. Two days later they issued our clothing. I took a liking to a boy named Smitty. His full name was Smitty Smith. We put on our fatigues and green caps, turned the bills up, and headed to the P.X. We met a little man who was wearing all kinds of ribbons and medals. Smitty said loud enough for him to hear, "Boy, he is a sharp old gent." Well, the guy turned out to be Colonel Pratt, commander at the post. He hollered at us and asked us how long we had been in the Army. We told him two days. He motioned to Corporal Thornne and barked, "Let these young men know they are in the Army!"

Corporal Thornne took us over to a big pile of leaves and made us load up two wheelbarrows, push them about two and a half miles, and dump them. Then he made us reload the wheelbarrows, haul them back, and dump the leaves where we had picked them up the first time. Being a grown man with average intelligence, I thought that was a waste of valuable time. It made me mad and I just *had* to talk back. It took me a while to realize I *had* to take orders. Eventually I learned to keep my mouth shut and do what I was told.

Going on a Bivouac

I had another buddy named Joe Brown. His folks had a furniture store in Little Rock. Joe and I got loaded one night and had to go on a bivouac (a thirty-mile hike with just enough food to survive on). We had walked about a mile when Joe passed out on the side of the road. The cook's truck came by and picked Joe up. When the truck came by my squad, Joe Brown was sitting up there grinning and waving bye-bye to me and the others.

It wasn't easy, but I made it all the way to the thirty-mile point of the hike. A short guy was marching in front of me and I kept saying to myself, "If that scrawny little runt can make it, I can too." We got to the bivouac area and they made us dig a trench large enough to lie down in. I was tired and my head was throbbing. I found a trench that had been dug and filled back up, so I just scooped the loose dirt out of it. Then I went into my tent and went to sleep. Lieutenant Fodder tapped me on my boots and sarcastically said, "That's a nice trench you dug. It was quick."

I replied, "Yes sir. I was raised on a farm and I know how to use a shovel and pick."

"Is that right? Well, you dig another one right here. (Lieutenant Fodder pointed to the rockiest place in sight.) Someone may have used the bathroom in the one you scooped out, and you wouldn't want to lay down in it." I dug nearly all night, then had to march with the squad the next day.

Shooting Bull's Eye

I made it through training and made expert at shooting a rifle. At first they made me wrap a sling around my elbow, and I couldn't hit anything. Captain Hewston was a country boy from Georgia and he understood the situation. He said, "Private Reed, your shooting (he called it "marksmanship") is very bad," and I replied, "Sir, if they'd let me shoot this target the way I shoot squirrels at home, I could get bull's eye." He grinned and said, "Okay, shoot." I shot four bull's eyes in a row, and Captain Hewston told them to let me fire in my own fashion from then on.

Preparing for Inspection

Captain Hewston was a good man. One day he announced that General Sniff was coming for inspection of our company. The work detail was set up. Captain Hewston told me to cut hair in the dayroom, where they sent me one man at a time. I cut hair nearly all night. The next morning at revelry I was so tired I had trouble standing up, so Captain Hewston punched me in the tummy and told me to go and get some sleep. When General Sniff arrived, he didn't even bother to get out of his limousine. He just drove around. Boy, what a bunch of mad guys!

Army Days in Europe

After a few weeks of training I was sent overseas as an Infantry Rifleman Replacement. Our second child, Jim (named James Monroe after both grandfathers), was twelve weeks old the day I shipped out for Germany. I went overseas on the *Transport General Brook* with 3800 troops and ship's crew.

Things were very messy over there. I was issued a new rifle and full field equipment, then sent to a combat outfit. The unit moved every few days. I was in the combat outfit thirty-four days. I had two pairs of hand clippers, combs, and shears with me, so I cut hair every chance I got.

Using My Survivors

One day I sat a guy down on an ammunition box and cut his hair during our break. The Company Commander came by, saw it, and remarked, "Soldier, that is a good haircut. Were you a barber in civilian life?" I replied that I was, so he told me to come to the office. The Company Commander took my new rifle and equipment, then gave me a .45 pistol and two suits of clothes. Five days later I was dropped off at the 7th army headquarters as Company Barber. I was soon made section leader at the Company Barber Shop and spent the rest of my army life in Heidelburg. I will always believe being a barber saved my life. I still have my old Brown & Shop hand clippers which I used over there. I call them "survivors."

Seeing a Friendly Face from Home

The company barber shop was located by the main gate. One day I was standing by the main gate when a jeep pulled up. I recognized the driver, Roy Forest, from Plainview, Arkansas. We had grown up together as children.

(I was best man at his wedding and he was best man at mine.) It sure was good to see a familiar, friendly face!

Cutting Abe Lincoln's Hair

In Augsburg, Germany, just before the war ended, I cut a very tall gentleman's hair who had on an officer's uniform. He looked in the mirror when I got through and said, "Barber, I don't get that good a haircut in New York." He gave me a *big* tip—five whole dollars!

My next customer was a captain. When he sat in my chair he grinned and remarked, "You have something to write home about: You just cut Abe Lincoln's hair."

Thinking he was joshing me, I replied, "You're just trying to make me feel good."

The captain asked, "Seriously—do you know who that guy was? That was Raymond Massive, the actor who played Abraham Lincoln in the movie!"

Seeing a U.S.O. Show and Returning to the U.S.A.

After the war was over I went to an open air theater in Heidelberg and saw Jack Benny, Ingrid Bergman, Larry Adler, and Martha Tilton put on a USO show. Their entertainment was tops!

Army Days

     I came back to the United States in April of 1946. I returned to New York on a big transport named *Thomas Berry*. We were in storms for five days. I was sent to Camp Kilmer, New Jersey after landing in the New York harbor right in front of the Statue of Liberty.

❖ **5** ❖

❖ 5 ❖

HOME FROM THE ARMY

When I came home from Germany, my son Jim was walking and talking. He wouldn't have anything to do with me. Oh well, I don't hold that against him. I took his bedfellow. Three weeks after I got home Jim crawled up on my lap and showed me his favorite toy—a pretty red car. Considering that he only showed it to his best friends, I took it that Jim had decided to let me stay.

I took a short vacation before returning to work. I caught up on some fishing with Clebert, my wife's brother.

Working in Arkansas

Not long after my return from the Army, I bought a barber shop from a man in Fourche

Valley. He sold me his barber shop and building, then backed out on the deal. He backed out on the deal in order to rent two rooms upstairs to the Forrest Service for forty dollars per month. I saw and talked to the man one time after that, trying to get him to go up on haircuts. It hurts to lose confidence in someone you thought was a good person.

Next I bought a barber shop, a building, and two lots of land at Ola, Arkansas. One year later I sold the barber shop and doubled my money on it, then moved back to Dumas. I finally realized it was foolish to pay another barber forty cents out of every dollar I took in when I could have my own shop. This was when our third baby, Michael Dilon, came along. We called him Mike.

We lived at Dumas until 1952. I had quit the O.K. Barber Shop, so Joe Mitchell and I put in a new shop together. We put an air conditioner in it and soon we had all the business we could do.

In the evenings I still wanted to play baseball. Lillian felt like I had too much responsibility to be out playing ball, because I was now a grown man with a family to support. She told me that if I hurt myself, I would still have to go to work. I told her not to worry, because that wouldn't happen. Naturally, it was only a matter of days after that discussion that I made a baseball play which injured my ankle. I had to stand on one foot for two weeks while I cut hair.

Working in California

I still had the problem of breathing through the right side of my nose. I got sick and was told by my doctor that if I wanted to live very long, I should move to a hot, dry climate. I moved to California and got a job as a ranch foreman for the Maulhardt ranches in Oxnard, California.

Being sick with the breathing problem, I had to get out of the dust and fog. A sweet sister-in-law, Berline Patton, put in a good word for me and I got a job in Fresno, California with a school district. Later I was assigned to the Fresno City Schools as a Director of Operations. I supervised transportation, building maintenance and custodians, landscape maintenance, warehousing, and pest control. I went into school work May, 1954 and left May, 1965. When the school district replaced me, they had to hire two individuals.

❖ **6** ❖

Figure 6.1 "Children's Toys"

❖ 6 ❖

RAISING OUR CHILDREN

Raising Our Children in Arkansas

Chocolate Pie Stories

One day when our children were small, I got onto Mike about misbehaving. I asked, "Who do you like best, Mom and Dad or Uncle Ben and Miss Ida?"

Mike replied, "Uncle Ben and Miss Ida, and I want to go live with them." So I packed him some clothes in his little satchel and gave him his little purple-and-gold football jacket. Then Mike went to Ben's and Ida's and knocked on the door and said, "My daddy 'runded me off,' and I came to live with you and Miss Ida."

They took Mike inside, and when I went over to get him later, Uncle Ben had Mike on his knee feeding him chocolate pie. Mike wouldn't go home for several hours.

When Jim was about four years old, he went to Aunt Inez's and Uncle Herman's to visit. Aunt Inez gave him a piece of chocolate pie. Jim ate it, licked his lips, and suggested hopefully, "Aunt Inez, if my mommy were here, she would want me to have another piece of that pie." Inez and I still laugh about that.

A Cutie, a Charmer, and a Runaway Child

When Bunny was just old enough to talk, a friend of mine would come over, josh her up and down on his knees, and say, "You favor your daddy, but you have your mother's features." One day the preacher came to our house. He put Bunny on his knee and said, "You are a *cutie*," and she replied, "Yes. I favor my daddy, but I've got my mama's fixtures."

One day Miss Ida was walking down College Street in Dumas, Arkansas. She was returning home from her weekly trip to the beauty shop. Lillian and our children were in our front yard. Lillian saw Miss Ida and remarked pleasantly, "Miss Ida, your hair looks so nice."

Seven-year-old Bunny added, "Yes, Miss Ida, your hair *really* looks nice."

Jim, the four-year-old charmer, declared emphatically, "Miss Ida, you just look nice *all* over!"

❖   ❖   ❖

When Jim was a little-bitty tyke (about two years old), we lived a few houses away from my sister, Ola. Jim would go to Ola's house frequently, and Bunny would have to go retrieve him. It seemed like Jim was running away three to four times a day. After making one of her many trips, Bunny put her hands on her hips and announced in her strongest five-year-old voice, "I'll be *so* glad when I get this child raised!"

Raising Our Children in California

When our children were little, we went to the Bakers' Ranch in Camptinville, California near Grass Valley for a one-week vacation. The Bakers knew Lillian from the Baptist head-quarters in Fresno, and they invited us up for a week in one of their cabins. I guess it was one of the best vacations we ever had.

We had a little boat that Mr. Baker put in a small lake near our cabin. There were rainbow trout and a lot of bullfrogs in the lake. I fashioned a bow and some arrows, then attached a table fork to an arrow with a string. We found a spotlight and took turns shooting frogs. The boys got some and I got several. Bunny just shot the bullfrogs hard enough to make them jump. We had trout and frog legs for dinner.

A windy fellow named Duke worked for Mr. Baker. I think about all this guy did was kill ground squirrels, which were a nuisance on the ranch. Duke had our children scared to stick a foot out of the cabin after dark—he told them he'd seen a huge rattlesnake go under the cabin.

Bunny was always active in some kind of school program at Clovis High School. She was "Amy" in the play *Little Women*. She was very involved in her school, and a lot of cute boys liked her.

I will never forget one boy named Larry Schmidt. At first Larry hung around because he liked Bunny. Eventually, it turned out that instead of staying in town on weekends and being with Bunny, he came to Pine Flat Lake where Jim, Mike, and I camped. Larry would sharpen a stick, take a flashlight, and get us a mess of bullfrogs. Then I would cook frog legs (we all liked them).

Bringing Our Children for Visits

We brought our children back to Arkansas about every two years to see their grandparents, uncles, aunts, and cousins. When it was time to leave Papaw Woods' house, Papaw Woods gave each of our children a quarter. On one occasion, Jim bought a coke and a candy bar with his quarter. He had a dime and a nickel left over (the coke and the candy bar each had cost a nickel). Jim talked Mike into trading money, because Jim had two pieces of money and Mike had only one. Well, Mike traded with him. Before we got home, Jim had lost his quarter and he cried.

I seldom spanked our children. I loved them and talked to them. If they didn't straighten up, I made them go to bed, and I think that hurt them more.

❖ **7** ❖

❖ 7 ❖

BACK TO ARKANSAS

In 1965 I decided on what I guess was the best move I ever made. We returned to Arkansas. Lillian and I had a beauty shop and barber shop in Hot Springs, Arkansas from 1965 to 1980, when I retired on my sixty-second birthday.

Camping at Iron Creek

My oldest brother, Roy, had two children, Roy E. and Hattie Pearl. Roy E. and I had a lot in common. We both liked to hunt, fish, and tell good stories.

Roy E. turned out to be a journalist. He was a reporter for the *Arkansas Gazette* for about ten years, then was with the *New York Times* for about twenty years. He was the Southern Correspondent for the *Times* until about ten years ago. At that time he moved to Hog-eye, Arkansas and built a house which was featured in *Southern Living* magazine. He taught journalism at the University of Arkansas at Fayetteville. (He is now a freelance writer and author of several books.)

One time in the late 'sixties Roy E. kind of burned out on work, so he took some time off. He went to his mother's at Hot Springs and called me. Roy E. wanted me to take him camping and fishing up on Iron Creek, where he had lived as a child. We took my camper and boat and camped at the old Fortner hole, the biggest hole on Iron Creek.

The funny part of this story was that Roy E.'s mother told me her son was a health-nut and she didn't think I could get him to eat anything. I have always been a big eater, so I took plenty of good food. I'm not bragging, but I *am* a good cook. My mother was in bed sick for a long time in 1936, and she taught me how to cook. It comes in handy now, because Lillian got tired of cooking all these years. If we get anything to eat around our house these days, I have to cook it. Lillian tells me that what I mess up she will clean up (a fair deal, all in all).

Well, the first afternoon we caught nine big goggle perch. I cooked all nine fish, then made hush puppies. I also fried a skillet of potatoes and sliced a big onion, and guess what? "Wowo," as we called Roy E., ate seven of the nine fish and more than his share of potatoes and hush puppies. The next morning I cooked two slices of ham that were so big I had to make two cookings of it. I also made some eggs, hash browns, and biscuits with butter and sorghum molasses. Roy E. helped me polish off all of it.

Later, Roy E. and I went fishing again. (The weather was so fine that we absolutely couldn't resist.) While we were "suffering" in the lazy afternoon breeze, something kept making a big noise in the water behind us. We thought someone was throwing big rocks in the water off of a high rocky bank, but it turned out to be beavers. I guess they had babies and wanted to scare us off. The wildest thing was a constant ringing in the timber and it had us wondering if we were going crazy. We found out it was locusts. I have been told they come every thirteen years.

We had lots of time to relax and talk during our camping trip—especially when we went fishing. During our trip I found out Roy E. was jealous of me for two things: marrying Lillian and playing the fiddle. Roy E. was jealous of me for marrying Lillian because he had fallen in love with Lillian when he was just a child. Roy E. said he wanted to marry a girl just like her. (When Roy E. grew up he met Norma. They raised Johnny and Cinda and have several grand-children.)

Roy E. was also jealous of me because I could play the fiddle and he couldn't. He was always quick to remind me when I missed a note.

Actually, I don't know one note from another. I just play by ear. Uncle Albert, Dad's youngest brother, played an old fiddle (though he'd been blind from the age of eighteen). He taught me a few tunes. When Uncle Albert died at age seventy-four, he left the fiddle to me. (When I'm through with the fiddle, I want my daughter, Bunny, to have it.)

Missing a Scoop and Catching a Story

Roy E. and I moved our camper to the Afton Ratlif hole. We were fishing and listening to the crows holler and the calves bawl, when all of a sudden someone hollered, "Who are you for for president, Rube?"

I hollered back, "Wallace!"

"He's just been shot," the man said, then turned and walked back to his house. The voice was Afton Ratlif's. Afton was a man of few words.

Roy E. missed out on a good story about Wallace, but I really believe he wouldn't have traded that camping and fishing trip for many stories. He wrote a book and has that story in it.

❖　❖　❖

When we got back to Hot Springs after our camping trip, Roy E.'s mother asked me if I could get her son, the healthnut, to eat anything. I just grinned in front of Roy E. and answered, "A little."

Finding an Old Friend

One day my daughter, Bunny, my wife, Lillian, and I were in Dardnell, Arkansas. I had lost touch with Jimmy Ladd, my best childhood friend from Tippey Town, for about fifty years. I found out Jimmy had a furniture store in Dardnell. I asked my daughter to go into the furniture store and find Mr. Ladd. When Bunny found him, she said, "Mr. Ladd, my daddy wanted to come by and see if you had a good chair or mattress that you'd trade for an old shotgun."

Jimmy looked befuzzled for a split second, then laughed and asked Bunny, "Are you Rubin Reed's daughter?" She replied that she was, then we all had a good chuckle. We had a wonderful reunion.

❖ **8** ❖

Figure 8.1 "Fishing with Lillian"

❖ 8 ❖

RETIREMENT

Moving Home to Stay

I retired on my 62nd birthday in 1980. My brother-in-law and sister-in-law, George and Berline Patton, sold us five acres and the old house where all the Wood children were raised in Bluffton, Arkansas. We have been very happy here and we plan to stay.

Lillian has a map she drew of all our moves since we have been married. She says I moved her seventeen times. I tell Lillian I just married her and took her on an extended tour for forty years, then brought her back home. I don't know of another wife who has had that long and as pleasant a tour.

Hunting and Fishing

When I retired, I bought myself some bib overalls, two beagle hounds, and a Brittney Spaniel bird dog. I have enjoyed the Brittney more than any dog I've ever had. I have caught many birds with her.

Lillian says we have a perfect place to live. We have a pretty view of the mountains and I have a very good garden spot. I have never failed to grow enough for two or three families. My nephew, Butch Patton, lets me use his tractor and I grow a lot of vegetables. We have a pickup, a camper, and a good fishing boat. We do a lot of fishing. Lillian has been my main fishing buddy for many years. The only bad part is, she usually catches more fish than I do.

Surviving Health Problems

I was as healthy as an old horse until the third day of March in 1989. I had two strokes and almost died. I couldn't walk, talk, urinate, swallow, or move for seven and a half days.

I finally came out of it and can do about anything I want to except lift a lot and stoop over in the hot sun. I'm very fortunate that I didn't come out carrying a hand, dragging a foot, looking twisted in the face, or being slurred in my speech. It took me a long time to learn to walk again. I will never believe anything else but that the Lord saved my life so I could come home and take care of Lillian, who is sweet, kind, good, and pleasant.

❖ **9** ❖

❖ 9 ❖

FAMILY GET-TOGETHERS

A Special 50th Wedding Anniversary

The last and best joke I ever heard Dad tell was on his and Mother's 50th wedding anniversary. About sixty people were at the celebration. Dad had all the men-folks out under his big shade tree when he told this story:

Uncle Bert and Aunt Bessie were celebrating their 50th anniversary, and Uncle Bert and Aunt Bessie never had any children. A big nephew asked, "Uncle Bert, we have always wondered why you and Aunt Bessie never had any children. Why?"

Uncle Bert replied, "Well, two days before Bessie and I were to be married, we were riding down the road in a buggy. It began to rain, so I tied the horse up and we ran into an old hay barn. I guess I got the wrong idea. I hugged and kissed Bessie and said, 'Honey, since we're to be married day after tomorrow, why don't we just get a little headstart now?' It made her so mad, I just never did mention it to her again!"

❖   ❖   ❖

My father-in-law told another funny story. It went like this:

A woman flagged down a bus and got on. Pets were not allowed on the bus. The bus rolled along, when all of a sudden a puppy poked its head out of the top of her blouse. The woman was embarrassed and said in a loud voice, "A friend gave it to me, but she didn't tell me it wasn't weaned."

1991 Reed Family Reunion

The highlight of the year for us was April 6, 1991. We had a family reunion. Dad would have been one hundred and nineteen years old on that day. There were one hundred and twenty-seven people at the reunion, and only six of them were not kinfolks. Lena Reed Wehunt, my "baby sister," stated that whenever she shares with friends that she is from a family of eleven, people always respond by asking, "Were your parents Catholics?" to which she replies, "No, they were just sexy Baptists."

My brother, Bill, summed it up best. He looked around at the huge family gathering and said, "Boy, look at what Mom and Dad started on a rainy day!"

AFTERWORD

If there's one thing I'm proud of, it's this: In all the places Lillian and I have lived, we've always made friends with good people, and we've been able to keep our friends during all of our fifty-eight year tour. God has richly blessed us with fine friends and fine family, and we are very grateful to Him for that.

ABOUT THE CO-AUTHORS

Rubin Reed

Rubin Reed was born in 1918 and presently resides in Plainview, Arkansas. Rube is married to Lillian Wood Reed and is the father of three children: Bunny, Jim, and Mike. Rube has four grandchildren and nine great-grandchildren.

Rube has been a farmer, a barber, a ranch foreman, and a school administrator. As a master gardener, Rube has been featured in several local newspapers. (He's even had his picture in the paper for growing a seven-pound turnip!) Rube is a World War II Veteran and a Baptist Deacon.

Bunny Reed Woods

Bunny Reed Woods lives with her husband, Gary Woods, in Brentwood, Tennessee. Bunny is the mother of one son, Nathan. She also enjoys her four step-children and six grandchildren.

Bunny holds her bachelors degree from Fresno State University and her masters degree from Hampton University. She is an elementary school teacher who is known for telling her "Cotton-top Stories." Bunny has also been actively involved in Toastmasters International for twenty-one years.